PRAYERS
FOR OCD

T0169329

Also by Fay Sampson:

Prayers for Dementia: And how to live well with it

Prayers for Depression: And how best to live with it

Prayers for Anxiety: And how best to cope with it

PRAYERS
FOR OCD
Understanding and healing

FAY SAMPSON

DARTON · LONGMAN + TODD

First published in Great Britain in 2018 by
Darton, Longman and Todd Ltd
1 Spencer Court
140–142 Wandsworth High Street
London SW18 4JJ

© 2018 Fay Sampson

The right of Fay Sampson to be identified as the Author
of this work has been asserted in accordance with the
Copyright, Designs and Patents Act 1988.

ISBN 978-0-232-53368-2

A catalogue record for this book is available from the
British Library.

www.faysampson.co.uk

Designed and produced by Judy Linard
Printed and bound in Great Britain
by Bell and Bain, Glasgow

ABOUT THIS BOOK

Obsessive Compulsive Disorder (OCD) is not well understood by most people. It is sometimes the subject of jokes.

To those who suffer it, it is definitely no laughing matter. It can jeopardise your job, your relationships and gives you no peace of mind.

This book seeks to shed light on the condition, both for those who have it and for others. Its pages explore different aspects of the condition and its treatment. Each one is accompanied by a prayer.

The book is divided into two sections. Part A is for those with OCD, Part B for family, friends and the wider community.

When praying for someone, you may wish to insert their name, or the pronoun 'he' or 'she'.

There is a list of resources at the end, and pages for your own prayers.

I am deeply indebted to the many organisations whose wisdom has informed this book: particularly OCD-UK, OCD Action, Beyond OCD, Mind. You will find much more on their websites. I am grateful too for those who have shared their own experience of OCD and how they cope with it.

Half the royalties from this book will go to OCD-UK.

Peace I leave with you;
my peace I give to you …
Let not your hearts be troubled,
neither let them be afraid.

John 14:27

PART A

For the use of, or on behalf of, those with OCD

OBSESSIVE COMPULSIVE DISORDER

As children many of us skipped along the pavement, knowing that we mustn't step on the cracks. We couldn't have said what would happen if we did; we just enjoyed the shiver of excitement. That was a harmless superstition. But some people find their lives destroyed by a compulsion to do or avoid doing something. This is OCD, Obsessive Compulsive Disorder. There is nothing enjoyable about it.

Obsessions are thoughts that torment you. Typically, you fear you are going to harm someone you love.

This leads to compulsive behaviour. You may hide every knife and pair of scissors. Or you're fanatical about cleaning away germs. You may get up multiple times in the night to make sure you've locked the door or unplugged the iron.

It is sometimes called 'the doubting disease'. You have lost faith in yourself.

Be reassured. These thoughts are so repugnant to you that there is not the slightest danger that you will act on them. You are the last person who would harm the ones you love.

Your logical mind can know this, but it doesn't take away that awful obsessive thought and the compulsive behaviour that goes with it.

Christ of the understanding heart,

Only you know the fear that drives me.

I know that what I do seems ridiculous to the people around me. They find it hard to keep their patience with me.

I know too that it's ruining my life. A life you intended to be spent on better things.

I can't help myself. You see deep into my heart. You alone see the terrible thoughts that drive my compulsive behaviour.

I have to find a way out of this. It seems like moving a mountain to get rid of the obsessive thoughts which dominate my life and compel my actions.

Grant me a vision of a life free from my obsessions and compulsive behaviour. May I truly believe how wonderful that life would be.

Take me by the hand and lead me to the place of healing.

OBSESSIONS

What most people notice about OCD is the compulsive behaviour it gives rise to. You go through repeated rituals: washing hands, constantly asking for reassurance that you haven't harmed someone, and so on.

These compulsions are the result of frightening thoughts that obsess you. You fear you are going to damage someone you love, or even a stranger. This may be by physically attacking them, inappropriate sexual behaviour, poisoning them by poor hygiene. It's not just a low-level worry. To 'obsess' means to 'besiege'. These fears haunt you day and night. They cause you anguish. You have an overwhelming sense of your responsibility and the size of the threat.

If you are religious, you may be shocked by blasphemous thoughts. Or you may be besieged by the fear that you are going to stab someone.

It makes you want to do everything you can to avert that harm. You keep going over your car journey in your mind. Did you hit somebody? You repeatedly check your clothes for contamination. You may avoid contact with your child because you are afraid of abusing them.

There are no recorded cases of someone with OCD acting upon their frightening thoughts.

Holy Spirit, Comforter,

I come to you in horror at my own unworthiness.

Day and night, images come to me of causing harm, even death, to the ones around me. I can hardly bear to live with myself.

I do everything I can, over and over again, to make sure this doesn't happen. But the terrible thoughts won't go away. Day after day, they besiege me. No matter how often I repeat my rituals, it doesn't make things any better.

Spirit of Wisdom, there is a saner part of my mind which knows this is out of proportion, that it's ruining my life, that I have to change it.

You alone know how ashamed I am. How difficult it is to confess these thoughts.

I know I should see my doctor, but I dread what I have to tell them.

Surround me with your strength and love. Sustain me with the courage to say what I must.

COMPULSIONS

Obsessive thoughts lead to compulsive behaviours to ward off the things we fear.

They may have an obvious connection with the fear, like repeatedly washing hands or clothes. Or they may seem more like a superstitious ritual: touching things in a particular order, counting up to a certain number. You know it's illogical, but you feel something bad will happen if you don't. Or you may want desperately to displace the shocking thoughts with some neutral activity.

Other compulsive behaviour happens internally. You have to keep checking your memory to see that what you fear didn't actually happen. You may keep asking others for reassurance.

These repetitions can be immensely time-consuming. They put a great strain on the people you live with. They may cause you to be late so often that you lose your job.

You may know all this, but it doesn't take away the absolute necessity you feel to go through these procedures time after time.

The sad thing is that this compulsive behaviour doesn't get rid of the original obsession; it reinforces it.

The good news is that OCD is treatable. You need to seek this help.

Lord, you walk the valley of the shadow with us.

You know the fears that haunt my waking hours, and that will not let me sleep.

I know that my compulsive behaviour seems ridiculous to others. They cannot understand why I must repeat the same actions over and over again.

They cannot see inside my soul to the dread that consumes me. They do not feel the fear that drives me to do everything in my power to ensure that I do not cause harm. They just think I am being unbelievably fussy.

Have mercy on me, Lord. Take away the terror that overwhelms and exhausts me. Part of me knows that what I do is unnecessary. That doesn't take away the obsessive thoughts that drive my behaviour, or the fear of what will happen if I leave these rituals undone.

I need help.

Take me to a place of healing.

CAUSES

The causes of OCD are not yet fully understood. It usually first manifests itself when the sufferer is young.

A genetic link seems possible. If someone in your family has this condition, you may adopt similar coping behaviour to manage your own anxieties.

Some have been abused or bullied. This leads them to bully themselves. They have low self-esteem. Obsessive thoughts crowd in, telling them they are no good, unlikeable. They resort to compulsive behaviour, trying to replace unworthiness by perfection, or rituals to drown out that inner condemnation.

Your brain may lack the ability to turn off a helpful behaviour, like washing your hands, once it has been done. You are obsessed by the illogical fear of what will happen if you stop.

Some believe that the cause is a deficiency of serotonin in the brain; others, that this is a result of the condition.

While stress is not necessarily the cause, it makes it worse. A trauma, such as a car accident, may trigger OCD.

Some children develop OCD after a severe streptococcal infection. This link is not yet understood.

Despite the uncertainty about the causes, treatment does work.

God of Wisdom,

I bless you for those who devote their lives to seeking the causes of OCD. Guide their endeavours. Lead them to understanding.

I thank you for the many involved in advocacy and fund-raising for a better understanding of OCD. I acknowledge with gratitude the help I have received for my own condition, in ways I may not even know. Make me part of that endeavour, so that others too may benefit.

I often feel in the grip of something too powerful to resist. Shine the light of your understanding upon my tortured mind. Convince me that these obsessions have a cause, that they are not merely the result of my unworthiness.

Guide others to the same understanding of my illness. I know I'm hard to live with, difficult to employ. Grant them the compassion which comes from being better informed.

Above all, Lord, I am eternally grateful for your understanding. You know, better than anyone else, what compels me. You forgive me. You believe in me.

HARM

OCD ruins your life.

If you cannot leave the house without checking the doors and windows multiple times, you are unlikely to be a good timekeeper. If you exhaust the patience of your employer, you may lose your job.

These compulsions are not only time-consuming, they can be exhausting. You may decide it is not worth the hassle, and give up on your social life.

The repeated checks can be internal. Maybe you are constantly obsessing over your relationship. 'Is this the right person for me?' 'Am I right for them?' 'How are things going between us?' Few romances can survive this constant scrutiny.

You may be terrified of harming your child, physically or sexually. You minimise your contact with them. The essential parent-child bond doesn't happen.

Compulsive washing can damage your skin. Your clothes wear out sooner than they should.

You can't get a good night's sleep, because you keep having to get up to check you've locked the doors or turned electrical equipment off.

You may avoid having visitors because of the rituals of cleaning up after them.

You become very hard to live with.

It doesn't have to be like this.

Comfort me, Lord.

My life is a mess. I'm in trouble at work. I'm losing my friends. My family relationships are breaking down. My health is suffering.

I feel I have been taken over by a malignant spell. I can see everything going wrong, but I can't stop it. Part of me knows that there is no sense in what I keep doing. Yet I feel powerless to change.

Nothing will take away the overwhelming thoughts that terrible things will happen because of me.

Reach out to me, Saviour, in the muddle and mess I am making of my life. I've let it go on far too long.

I feel as though I am bewitched. But you have the power to break this spell.

Take my arm. Give me the courage I need. Whisper in my ear that you and I can beat this together.

Hold me to the vision of what life could be like without this.

Lead me to those who can make that hope come true.

WE NEED TO TALK

The WHO (World Health Organisation) lists OCD among the ten most debilitating conditions. It seriously damages your lifestyle, spoils relationships and can lead to loss of earnings. It is treatable. Yet people typically wait 10-15 years before consulting their doctor.

You feel shame and embarrassment about your condition. Your obsessive thoughts tell you that you are a rotten person. You are horrified by the acts of harm you fear you will commit unless you go through with your compulsions. You despise yourself. You may even think yourself evil. It's hard to confess this to someone else.

What a needless waste of a life, when help is available.

If you take your courage in your hands and go to your doctor, the likelihood is that you will gain a sympathetic ear. It will help to write down beforehand what you want to say.

You should be told about the treatments available: talking therapies and/or medication.

Just occasionally, you may find a doctor who is not well-versed in this condition and does not take it seriously. OCD Action has an information card for GPs.

Alternatively, the NHS Choices website tells you how to refer yourself for psychological therapy services.

God, my Rock,

This is one of the hardest things I will ever have to do.

For years, I've let my obsessions and compulsions ruin my life. Now I hear you telling me it can't go on like this. I know it's true.

But I'm afraid. I feel so deeply ashamed of the thoughts I have. Thoughts of violence or sexual abuse. I hear a different voice telling me what a terrible person I am. How can I confess this to someone else?

Lay your steadying hand upon my shoulder. Convince me that this is an illness like any other. It can be treated.

It's hard to believe that, when I am so racked with dark thoughts.

I need all the courage you can give me. Take me by the hand and lead me.

I'm panicked about how I can put such things into words. Guide me how to set it down on paper, so that I don't fail to say what I need to.

Stand by me.

COGNITIVE BEHAVIOURAL THERAPY

OCD messes up your life. It harms your relationships, your job, your physical wellbeing. It causes you inner anguish.

It can be treated.

As with many mental illnesses, the best treatment is a talking one. In this case, it is Cognitive Behavioural Therapy (CBT).

Unlike many talking therapies, it does not delve into your past. Instead, it focuses on your present problems. OCD springs from negative thinking. Your therapist will help you to break down the condition into separate parts: thoughts, physical feelings, behaviour. When you agree on what is unhelpful, the two of you will work out how to change this. You may need to see your therapist for 5 to 20 sessions.

It can be emotional, as you relive agonising thoughts, but you will emerge with greater confidence and control over your life.

It's not a one-off. You can use these tools in future to guard against relapse.

CBT is free on the NHS, but there may be a waiting list. Or you can seek private treatment.

This method can also be applied in groups, through computer programs and self-help books.

Generous God,

I come to you with overwhelming gratitude. At last there is a way out, after all my years of suffering.

I bless you for the therapists, who make their wisdom and experience available to people like me. For the health service which makes this possible.

My life has been a night of negativity for so long. Now I see the beginning of dawn.

Give me the resolution to commit myself to treatment, the patience to wait until a therapist becomes available, the perseverance to continue, even though some sessions may be painful.

Lord, you know how many people like me wait years before seeking help. May I add my voice to those who are talking openly about OCD and encourage others like me to seek the healing available.

EXPOSURE AND RESPONSE PREVENTION

The widely recognised treatment for OCD is Cognitive Behavioural Therapy (CBT). This includes Exposure and Response Prevention (ERT). The sufferer is gradually introduced to things that trigger the obsession that plagues them. They are encouraged to reduce the compulsive behaviour associated with it.

If your compulsion is to wash your hands repeatedly, you may be asked to wait a while before you do it, and then gradually reduce the number of washes. Eventually, you wash only once. The calamity you feared doesn't happen. You are able to set a distance between the obsession and the behaviour you associated with it.

You will naturally shy away from triggering deliberately those terrifying thoughts. It takes courage and perseverance to face up to them and to break the link between the obsession and the compulsion. You need to be committed.

The reward is that your anxiety will gradually diminish as you defeat the ogres that have bullied you. The more you engaged in compulsive behaviour, the more it was reinforcing the belief that the danger you feared was real. You now show yourself that it was an illusion. You have stopped obeying the compulsion and the world hasn't come to an end.

Lord, who walked the valley of the shadow,

I'm scared.

Only you know the intensity of the dread that haunts me. I'm convinced that performing my rituals prevents something terrible from happening.

Now they want to deliberately trigger the thoughts I am most afraid of. Hold my hand while I trust myself to my therapist. Help me to confront the enormity of my fear.

These are going to have to be small steps. I really want to get rid of my compulsions, but I'm terrified of doing it all at once.

Part of me knows that the way I behave is irrational, but that doesn't take away the dread. I have this overwhelming fear that I am responsible. Suppose something bad happens because I don't obey my compulsions. I will be racked with guilt. Somehow, I have to sever this link between my fear and my actions. It will take all the courage I have.

You want me to be whole, to lead a normal life. Stand with me.

GENERALISED ANXIETY MEDICATION

It is generally agreed that the best treatment for OCD is Cognitive Behavioural Therapy (CBT). But there may be a long waiting list for CBT, and it's not right for everyone. Medication can help. It may be temporary, before therapy begins, or the two may be prescribed together, particularly if the condition is severe.

The most effective drugs are antidepressants. The recommended form is Selective Serotonin Reuptake Inhibitors (SSRIs). There are some possible side effects, but these usually wear off. Very rarely, the tablets can cause thoughts of suicide or self-harm. If this happens, contact your GP, or go immediately to A&E.

Don't expect an immediate cure. It may take weeks before you feel a positive effect from medication. Keep going for the prescribed period.

It may need some experimenting before your doctor finds the most effective drug, or combination of drugs, and the best dosage for you.

Always tell your doctor what other medicines you are taking, to make sure there are no adverse reactions. This includes herbal remedies.

Medication is not a total cure. What you want is to reduce the symptoms to a level where you can get on with the rest of your life.

Lord, you have a sense of humour,

You must smile as you look at me now with these tablets in my hand. For years I've been tormented by my obsessions. I've let my compulsions mess up my life. This life you gave me for something better than OCD.

And now, here I am, with the means for relief. I come to you with contrition for all the years I've wasted, because I was too ashamed and embarrassed to confess my terrible thoughts.

I bless you for giving me the courage to open up at last. For the understanding I have received from my doctor. For this offer of a way out.

I know it's not over yet. Between us, my doctor and I must find the right drug and dosage. It will not totally banish the monster in my mind. Give me strength and perseverance to go on co-operating with my healing.

Help me back to a life where I can serve you better.

RELIGION

You might think that having a religious faith would be a comfort for someone in the grip of OCD, but it's not necessarily so.

You may be assaulted by blasphemous thoughts which appal you. You resort to praying over and over again in an effort to wipe out your 'sin'. But the thoughts don't go away.

Be comforted. The very fact that you feel so terrible about this means that the obsession is not a reflection of your true nature. If it were, you would revel in these shocking thoughts.

Repetitive prayer may be one of the compulsions you feel driven to perform to ward off other obsessive thoughts. It's a compulsion that other people can't see, but it still consumes your life.

The prayers themselves may be a cause of anguish. You fear that you are not saying them correctly, or not performing religious rituals in the right way. You have to repeat them over and over in an effort to get them right.

You may be continually asking for forgiveness, directly from God, or through a member of the clergy. No reassurance is ever enough.

The truth is that medical treatment is the answer to your prayers.

Ever-Forgiving Saviour,

I fear I weary you with my incessant prayers. I'm racked with doubts that nothing I do is good enough. I can't even worship properly.

I know the people I confess to can't understand why I won't accept forgiveness. It's as if I don't have enough faith. Speak your wisdom to me. Calm this mental torture.

I do so want to be good. Over and over I accuse myself of breaking your rules. Can you not step in and change this?

Stop me, precious Lord. I can't go on like this. The faith that should be my greatest joy is now a source of torment.

Everything I've been taught tells me that prayer should be the answer. Yet prayer itself has become the burden.

Grant me the strength to listen to the voices that are telling me that healing for OCD comes through your human agents.

Bless me with the courage to go and seek the peace I so long for.

TIME OFF

More than 1 per cent of the population have OCD. Half these cases are severe. In the worst scenario, it can make you unemployable, ruin your social life and leave you no time to do the things you want to.

It's not that bad for everyone, or at all times. You can have good days, when you behave almost normally. You may wake and find that you've had a good night's sleep. Your compulsions may be of a type which remain largely hidden. OCD doesn't always take over the whole of your life.

Seize on these reprieves. Hang on to the vision that this is what life could really be like. Allow them to give you hope that your OCD can be manageable.

Remember that your worst fears didn't materialise when you had a day without rituals. If you can, cut back on your compulsive behaviour at other times too. Ration yourself to perhaps three checks on the locks, or three hand washes. Then get on with the rest of your life.

That's easier said than done. Your obsessive thoughts are real, the compulsion powerful. But the times when you survived without your rituals were real too. Don't let the monster win.

Lord of Refreshment and Serenity,

I thank you that there are times like today when the pressure eases for a little while. I realise that I have been getting on with my life without my compulsive rituals. I feel a weight has fallen from my shoulders.

But there is still a niggling guilt. What if harm does come because I didn't do what I usually do? Let me feel the grip of your hand telling me that all is well.

I know that tomorrow will probably be different. The fears may return in all their intensity, like a circling storm cloud. I will be driven to repeat those actions over and over again.

Grant me a vivid memory of today. Let me rejoice in recalling what it is like to live freely. May I cherish this precious gift, and use it to fight off the monster in my mind.

Help me to take this little piece of normal life and use it in your service.

PURE-O

We usually think of OCD as obsessively tidying things or washing hands.

Not all OCD shows itself through external behaviour. Sometimes it's all in the mind. You're obsessed by thoughts you hate. You desperately try to cancel these out by silently counting to a 'safe' number, repeating a rhyme or a prayer. You may repeatedly check your feelings towards a partner because you fear they are inappropriate.

This internal behaviour is called 'Pure-O', though it does involve compulsions as well as obsessions. They're just hidden.

You may avoid certain people, busy places, sharp instruments, routes home, because these are associated with what you dread.

Repetition and avoidance do not make the fear go away. The time you spend on these inner rituals can be just as destructive as obsessively checking door locks. The rest of your life is on hold.

You are so ashamed of your thoughts that it seems impossible to tell anyone about them. You may find it easier to talk to a faceless stranger on an OCD helpline. They know all about this condition. They won't judge you. They can ease the load and give you the advice you need.

Spirit of Silence and Inner Space,

You see where no one else does.

Inside my mind, I'm racked with thoughts that disgust me. I fear I'm an evil person, even to have such thoughts. Over and over, I go through my mental rituals to prevent myself doing harm. I can't concentrate on the things I should.

Reach out to me through the muddle and the torment. Speak your clear, calm voice of wisdom. I long for your reassurance that the person who dominates my thoughts is not really me.

Let me feel the nearness of your love. Give me hope that you believe in my potential goodness. Strike a shaft of light between me and that obsessive monster.

I'm ashamed to confess the thoughts I have. Grant me the humility to take them to someone who will listen with understanding.

I know that healing will require courage. Sooner or later I must face this monster and deny its right to take over my life. Fill me with your strength.

HOARDING

OCD can show itself in compulsive hoarding. You may feel you need to keep every issue of a newspaper or magazine. You're afraid that if you throw out just one, it will be the very one you need next week.

You may be a compulsive shopper, and unable to throw purchases away. Or you take things out of skips.

An experience of past deprivation may make you fear discarding anything that could be useful.

You may dread that someone will be injured or infected by something you throw out.

It may be that you have found objects more reliable recipients of your affection than people.

Hoarding is dangerous. Your home may become so crowded that you can hardly walk through it. You're embarrassed to have anyone enter it. It becomes a haven for vermin. It's a fire hazard. The structure may become unsafe.

A particularly distressing form of hoarding is keeping a large number of animals. You can't care properly for all of them.

You will probably get angry when others want you to throw things out. Yet your hoarding distresses you.

Take heart. Hoarding is not always caused by OCD, but it responds to the same treatment.

Christ, who abandoned all possessions,

You must wince when you look at the state of my home. I'm embarrassed even to let my friends see it.

I didn't mean to get into this state. I just can't stop collecting things and I'm too afraid to throw them out. Yet here I am, surrounded with towering piles of stuff. Even if I wanted something I know I have, I'd have no idea where to find it.

I know that those who love me are worried about this. What if there's a fire? Rats? What if the floor caves in? They urge me to get rid of things, even just a few at a time.

But I'm terrified to let go.

Lord of healing, you can lead me to a better place. You are holding out your hand to me. You know that I'm daunted by the colossal task of relinquishing all that I have.

Yet you gave up everything for me.

Help me.

BODY-FOCUSED OCD

Sometimes OCD shows itself through obsessive concentration on body parts. You find yourself obsessively swallowing or blinking. Breathing stops being something you do unconsciously; you can't help focusing on it. If you try to shift your attention away, anxiety mounts unbearably.

It can be any body part: pulse, fingers, the view of your nose when you read, eye floaters. You fear that, if you stop concentrating, these parts will not return to normal functioning.

You become obsessed about obsessing.

As with many forms of OCD, obsessive thoughts get in the way of normal living. You can't concentrate on work. You don't drop off to sleep. People think you're unsociable because you don't pay attention to what they're saying.

The clinical name for this is sensorimotor OCD. It seems most common among people who have a history of OCD or anxiety disorder.

Treatment involves uncoupling this sensory awareness from anxiety. The more anxious you are about thinking of something, the more likely you are to do it. Imagine being told not to think about an elephant.

You will be helped to become more relaxed and accepting.

Mindfulness is one way of paying attention to your body without critical judgment.

Creator Spirit, when the world was new you formed us, and you saw that it was good.

Help me to rejoice in the body you have given me, in all its beauty and imperfections.

Give me a trust in your life-giving grace. It does not need my anxiety to make me breathe, or see, or pump my blood. Let me relax into your loving care and get on with the life you have set before me.

Spirit of Freedom, loose me from the obsession that my life is being taken over by such obsessive thoughts. Let me not pile anxiety upon anxiety. Help me to let go and accept my body as it is. Free my mind for the service of your Kingdom.

Accept my gratitude for all you have given me: health, food, clothing, a home. Let me pray for those who do not have what their body needs, instead of worrying about my own.

Grant me your peace.

BABIES

Giving birth to a child should be a joyful time. But pregnancy and caring for a new baby can also be a challenge to mental health.

It's normal for a new mother to worry about caring for a baby. It's a big responsibility. But OCD can drive you to extremes. You may be obsessed by fears that you will harm your child by lack of hygiene. You sterilise equipment, wash your hands, clean their surroundings, repeatedly. You may limit the contact others have with your baby.

You check the baby throughout the night. You constantly seek reassurance.

You may be haunted by fears that you will abuse your newborn, violently or sexually. So you keep your contact with the baby to the minimum. You lose that precious bonding in those early weeks.

Fathers can also suffer from perinatal OCD. They feel an exaggerated sense of their responsibility for this child.

OCD often expresses itself as perfectionism. You feel you will not rest easy until everything is exactly right. This is true with your baby. No matter how often you perform your protective rituals, it never seems enough.

Your baby deserves better than this.

Seek help.

Fathering and Mothering God,

I come to you in distress. I longed for this baby, but now I feel overwhelmed by the responsibility.

I'm scared I will harm it, when that's the last thing I want. I worry it will die if I have a moment's lapse in cleanliness. I clean obsessively.

The worst thoughts are that I will be the one to harm it. I imagine myself lashing out at it when it cries. I could kill it.

Or I am horrified by sexual thoughts about my baby.

I go through rituals, reciting protective words or numbers. I'm sure something terrible will happen to my child if I don't.

Lord, I'm a mess. I knew that looking after a baby wouldn't be easy. I didn't expect this constant fear. It's taking away all the happiness I looked forward to.

Parenting God, take me in your mothering arms. A saner voice tells me this isn't good for my baby. Show me what to do.

STUDENTS

University can be stressful. If you have a tendency to OCD, this can trigger it.

You need to register with a GP. A larger practice is more likely to have someone well informed about OCD. They may even have a CBT therapist.

You will be told about the University Counselling Service.

It's also advisable to register with the university disability service. Your compulsions may mean you need extra time to complete an assignment or sit an exam. A note-taker may help if your attention wanders during lectures. An 'exam prompter', will help you concentrate.

You may be eligible for a Disabled Students Allowance. Seek advice.

It's best to share this with your personal tutor. With your consent, they can tell the people who need to know.

Don't be shy about confessing your condition to your fellow-students. You may find some of them are suffering too. Others are likely to be supportive.

If you don't get a sympathetic hearing, there are informative leaflets. See 'Resources'.

Make sure you get the sleep, diet and exercise you need. Make a sensible work plan, with breaks.

Students who disclosed their OCD late on, almost always wish now that they had done so sooner.

Creator of Exciting Possibilities,

This is an opportunity I may never have again. Please don't let my OCD mess it up.

I thank you that so much help is available. But I'm going to need courage. I feel such a rotten person that I'm ashamed to tell other people. I know things will be better if I do, but my heart is telling me something different from my head. I'm afraid. Hold my hand and lead me forward.

I will hardly need to tell the people I live with. They can see how oddly I behave. Help me to overcome the disgust OCD makes me feel about myself. Give me the wisdom to show them what it feels like, to point them to websites or show them leaflets. Use me to deepen understanding.

It's going to be hard. My obsessive thoughts get in the way of my work. My compulsions foul up my social life. Give me the blessing of friends and professionals to support me through this.

OCPD

A condition commonly confused with OCD is Obsessive Compulsive Personality Disorder (OCPD). You have a compulsive need for perfectionism, neatness and order. This is not to avert the harm that the OCD sufferer fears that they will cause others. It's a need to impose your sense of order on the world around you. You may feel self-righteous, and angry with those who don't comply with your standards.

You work hard, but your perfectionism gets in the way of completing a task. You can't delegate or share work, because you're sure it won't be properly done.

You put your work above your family. You find it difficult to make friends. You dislike spending money or throwing things out.

The trouble is that this condition makes it hard to admit that there is anything wrong with you.

If you can get over that hurdle and ask for help, then the treatment is similar to that for OCD. Cognitive Behavioural Therapy and medication with SSRIs can both help. The good news is that OCPD is one of the most treatable personality disorders.

This is a type of anxiety disorder. Find out about relaxation techniques. These will help to relieve your tension.

Righteous God,

I come to you in bewilderment. I've worked night and day to ensure that everything is done as well as possible. I demand the highest standards from those I work with. I've sacrificed my home life and friendships. How can this be wrong?

Yet people tell me I've got my priorities confused. They say my meticulous standards prevent me from delivering a result. That I'm not working well with my colleagues. I should delegate more.

I feel so tense when I think of relinquishing control. I can see so clearly what needs to be done.

Help me.

Do I really need to see a doctor? It would be an admission that something is wrong with me, when it seems to me that the fault is in other people.

Yet I confess that the burden of anxiety weighs me down. I don't enjoy life as other people do. I'm haunted by the fear that nothing I do is good enough.

Nerve me to take that difficult first step.

BODY FOCUSED REPETITIVE BEHAVIOURS

A significant number of people twist and pull their own hair, even breaking it or pulling it out. Others compulsively pick their skin. Some bite their cheeks or nails and or nose-pick.

These are Body Focused Repetitive Behaviours. They are most common in females. They can spoil your appearance and cause infection. You may avoid people, because you are ashamed of your bald patches or damaged skin.

It can happen without you being aware of it — while you are watching TV, for instance.

Its repetitive nature can make it look like OCD, but it is not. It's considered OCD-related.

Some of these actions, like squeezing spots, are a source of pleasure, which OCD compulsions are certainly not. But in the end it causes a deep sense of shame.

It becomes serious if it happens daily, and significantly damages your body.

There can be many causes. Anxiety makes it worse, but people without anxiety also suffer from it. For some, it's a certainty that there is something wrong with them, that needs to be removed. For others, it's a way of avoiding social situations. 'I can't go out looking like this.'

Treatment needs to be adapted to the individual.

Jesus, Word made Flesh,

I'm a mess. I've damaged my body to the point where I am ashamed to let other people see.

I don't know why I do it, but I can't seem to stop. It can happen while I'm doing something else, like using my computer.

It's like an addiction that I can't break free from. I even get a twisted sort of pleasure from it. Hold me back.

Lord of Incarnation, you can see the harm I'm doing to the body you gave me. Help me to respect and honour your gift.

Grant me honesty to face what is wrong with me. Lift the burden of shame I feel about myself. I know there is help available. Give me the courage to seek it.

Make me whole.

OUTCOMES

It is perhaps too much to hope for a complete cure for OCD. Research is on-going. But the majority of people who have treatment report a major improvement in their quality of life.

They may still be visited by unwelcome thoughts, but they have learned how to stand up to them and set a distance between the fear and the compulsions. Or they may perform that behaviour a few times and then say, 'That's enough'. They get to work on time, enjoy a social life, get a good night's sleep.

The cruel thing about OCD is that it makes you feel guilty and ashamed, so you are afraid to tell anyone. People often develop it as children, yet are well into adulthood before they seek help. They suffer needless pain and waste many years of their lives.

The benefits of talking therapy don't end when the course is finished. You will learn strategies to cope with those bullying thoughts in future. You will be able to disconnect them from the ritualistic behaviour. You get back control of your life.

Success rates are high, but not 100 per cent. The sooner treatment begins, the better the prospects of recovery.

Liberating God,

I come to you in overwhelming gratitude for this release.

My monster still visits me, but now I have the courage to say 'No'. It no longer takes up hours of my day. I've got my life back.

Thank you for the freedom you have restored to me. For the organisations that provided me with advice. For the friends and family who encouraged me to seek help. For the doctors and therapists who work to heal people like me. For those conducting research, so that more sufferers may benefit.

I still need you beside me. There are things I couldn't do because of my OCD. Now I have to learn my way in an unfamiliar world.

I pray for all those still in the grip of their fears. Those too ashamed to talk to anyone. Those who do not realise that treatment is available.

Bless the work of all those who hold out a hand to them.

May I use my voice to bring liberation to others.

PART B

For the use of family, friends
and the wider community

'A BIT OCD'

One of the things that causes great pain to OCD sufferers is to hear someone say: 'I'm a bit OCD'. They mean that they are particular about keeping their desk tidy or wiping the kitchen surfaces with disinfectant. It's said humorously.

Real OCD is anything but a joke. It causes the sufferer anguish. It ruins lives.

Never make fun of any mental illness. It creates an almost unbridgeable gap between those who have the condition and those who don't. OCD sufferers are already in distress. They need understanding. Hearing jokes made about their obsessive compulsive behaviour leads to feelings of isolation, even despair.

Instead, find out all you can about this painful condition. Be on the alert for those who genuinely have OCD, and are not just fussy about neatness or hygiene. These are people whose lives are taken over by their obsessive thoughts and the rituals they are driven to perform again and again.

Find out all you can about the condition and how to respond to it. This book is intended to deepen understanding. You will find many more helpful sources at the end of this book.

Discover how you can help.

Jesus, Lord of Compassion,

You saw into the hearts of those who came to you for help. You knew the anguish they carried daily. You held out the comfort of your healing love.

I confess my own thoughtlessness. I've made jokes like, 'I'm a bit OCD about this', when all I meant was that I'm fussy about doing something. This is an aspect of my life that has never caused me pain, yet I've used it as a cheap excuse for humour.

It never occurred to me that someone else might be deeply hurt by my light-hearted words.

I come to you in contrition. I didn't mean to wound anyone. I just didn't think.

Help me to see beneath the careless joke, to find out all I can about OCD. Show me what I can do to help, even if it is only to persuade others not to cause pain like this.

Fill me with your heart of compassion for those who suffer anguish daily from this illness.

CO-OPERATING WITH OCD

The two of you are getting ready to go out. You're standing at the door waiting, while the other is going through the seemingly endless ritual of checking all the doors and windows, over and over again.

Your heart aches for them. You want to relieve the pressure.

Or you are looking at your watch and fuming with impatience. You are going to be late, again.

Either way, you offer help. 'Let me check upstairs, while you do downstairs.'

Don't. Whatever your reasons for offering, you are reinforcing the idea that these rituals are necessary. It's essential that someone with OCD realises that this behaviour is out of touch with reality. It's ruining their life.

Things are not going to get better until they seek help. Co-operating with rituals will only delay that moment.

In any case, your help is unlikely to take away the compulsion they feel to double check every door and window for themselves.

You may have to leave without them.

It can be tough on both of you. But the one you love needs to confront reality.

The best thing you can do is to help them make an appointment to see their doctor.

Christ, who walked the hard way,

You know how much I ache for the one I love who has OCD. I desperately want to help. I can see how this is messing up their life.

Yes, Lord, I'll be honest. It's messing up my life too. I try to be patient, but it's not easy. Too often, I let my impatience show. Forgive me, and make me kinder.

You warned your disciples you were taking them on a hard road. The wiser part of me knows that the road to recovery will be difficult. Grant me the strength to go against my natural instincts and refuse to co-operate with their obsessive behaviour.

Give me wisdom to see when I should no longer wait until the rituals are finished. It's hard for me to shut the door on them. It causes grief to both of us.

I need your courage, Lord. Make me strong and wise to lead the one I love to where healing for OCD can be found.

HELP

It's distressing to see someone you care about in the grip of OCD. You desperately want to help.

You've been told that sharing compulsive rituals is wrong. It only validates the obsession. So what can you do?

The most supportive thing is to encourage the one you love to talk about their obsessive thoughts. This is not easy. They probably feel ashamed of their conviction that they will cause harm. Listen sympathetically. Don't sound judgemental. Confessing their thoughts to you will make it easier to tell their doctor.

Encourage this. They will find it hard, but the sooner they do, the better.

You can't force the issue. Some people contact a mental health charity on the sufferer's behalf, without their consent. They may make an appointment with the doctor behind their back. People have even asked how they can give their loved one medication without their knowledge.

Respect the integrity of the one you love. Effective treatment requires their informed cooperation.

You can obtain leaflets about OCD, or print out website advice. Show this to them. Discuss it. If they are reluctant, leave it for them to read in private. It will reinforce the need to see a doctor.

Caring Christ,

I so much want to help the one I love. My heart bleeds to see them in the grip of their obsessions.

Part of me wants to take over. If I can't get them to a doctor, I'm tempted to do it myself. I want to ring an OCD helpline and ask them to intervene.

Forgive me, Lord, for trying to force my will upon my loved one. You offered yourself to the world, but never forced anyone to believe.

Make me a sympathetic listener. Restrain me from scolding them for inappropriate thoughts. Let me assure them how much I love and respect them. How much you value them. Help me to show them how they exaggerate their responsibility for others' welfare.

I know that healing requires talking to a doctor. Teach me to understand how hard this will be. May I give them warm encouragement, but never bully them.

Daily, you give me your tender care. Make me the channel of your love.

FAMILY

If someone in the family has OCD, everyone is affected. Obsessive rituals slow life down. The sufferer may not want other people in the house. They may say no one else should use a particular piece of equipment.

It helps to sit down as a family and discuss this. Your instinct is to soothe the one you love by giving in to their obsessions. You need to say, gently, 'No. Your fears aren't real. We're not going along with this'. You can soften the negativity with a hug.

Assure them that you love and believe in them. Treatment is available. You will support them through it. Reassurance is particularly important if they suffer a relapse after treatment. Encourage them to continue with the coping exercises they have been taught.

OCD causes stress to all who live with it. It's natural to get cross at times. Be quick to ask forgiveness. Assure them that OCD is an illness; it's not their fault.

You will need resources of humour. Never mock OCD, but help the one who has it to see the gap between the unreality of their fears and the exaggerated lengths they feel driven to. That's worth a smile.

Christ, who calls all those who love him his family,

Cast your loving smile over us.

This is a hard road we have to walk. Let us walk it together. It's going to be tough to speak up for sanity, and yet to see the pain of the one we love. We so much want to take the pain away.

Guide us to come together and agree a plan. Let it be one that acknowledges the needs of all the family. Don't let OCD dominate life for all of us. Help us to go on believing that this will benefit the one who suffers from it, as well as us.

May I never lose sight of the other family members, and how this impacts on them. Show me how to balance conflicting needs.

Lord, you know how quick I can be to lose my temper when I'm frustrated. Forgive me. Help me to forgive myself. May we never lose the sense of humour we need to help us get through this.

CHILDREN

Over 2 per cent of children have OCD. It's not attention-seeking or a passing phase. The brain acts differently. Scary thoughts cause the child to perform physical or mental rituals in order to ward off harm. These can take more than an hour a day,

Your child may be unreasonably afraid of someone breaking in or of the house burning down. They constantly check that everything is safe. They may be so afraid of contamination that their hands are raw from washing. They may recite numbers or 'magic words'.

They have an exaggerated sense of their responsibility for causing harm.

It's not bad parenting which causes this. There may be a genetic link, but this is not fully understood. It can come on suddenly, even overnight.

OCD is treatable. Early diagnosis means better prospects of recovery. The treatment is as for adults: talking therapy and/or medication.

Assure your child that the obsessive thoughts are not the real 'them'. You may talk about the 'bully' or 'monster' in their head. Encourage them to draw a picture of it, to distance themselves.

Join a support group or online forum with other parents.

Levels of OCD can vary. Enjoy the good days.

Loving Father,

I expected problems with my child. Chickenpox, falling off a bike. I never anticipated this.

My heart aches to see them so obviously unhappy. Time and again they go through their rituals, yet the fear that causes them never seems to go away. I long to help.

Reassure me that OCD is treatable. Nerve me to take my child to see a doctor and to cooperate with their treatment.

Grant me wisdom as I seek to reassure my child that the monster in their head can be made to go away. May I give them the courage to stand up to it.

You know how embarrassed I feel when others notice it. Deepen my own understanding. Help me to be so well-informed about OCD that I can be an advocate for children like mine.

In my yearning to help, may I respect my child as a person. Give me the humility to consult them before discussing their OCD with others.

They are uniquely precious in your sight.

SCHOOL

With so many children suffering from OCD, every school should expect to have some cases.

The school may already be aware of some. There are symptoms to look for: obsessive arrangement of objects, prolonged toilet visits for cleanliness, repeatedly handing in work late because of compulsive rituals, poor attention caused by obsessive thoughts, tiredness through disturbed sleep, avoiding touching certain materials, fear of using a certain number, late arrival, over-meticulous handwriting, work with many corrections.

Avoid causing stress. Make sure the student is clear about the task required. Give advance warning of an unusual activity. If necessary, allow the use of a computer to remove anxiety over handwriting. You may need to relax the rules for dress code or toilet breaks.

OCD damages confidence and social relationships. Offer support and praise.

Be aware of bullying from other children.

Never punish the pupil for OCD behaviour. It's already deeply distressing.

It's very likely that the pupil's family will already be aware of their OCD. But some may never have heard of this condition. You may wish to talk to them about this child.

Respect the pupil. Keep them in the picture over any discussions you have.

Lord,

As if there weren't enough stresses in teaching already. Now they're wanting me to look out for cases of OCD. Do they know how many excuses there are for lateness, messy work, demands to go to the toilet?

All right. I'll calm down. I can hear your quiet voice telling me that each of my pupils is a precious child of God.

Grant me the patience and understanding to find out more about this condition. May I be concerned enough to share this with my colleagues.

Give me wisdom as I look at all these tangled young lives in my care. Help me to discern who might have OCD. May I examine their behaviour sympathetically.

Guide me to understand what it must be like to have this bully in your head, demanding such unreasonable behaviour. Help me walk the fine line between making the right allowances and reinforcing their compulsive behaviour.

In a crowded classroom, I am going to need wise judgement. Help me.

NOTICING

OCD is pretty obvious to the people who live with a sufferer, unless it's 'Pure-O', where it all happens internally. It may be harder to spot in a church or workplace.

If someone is persistently late, it may be because of time-consuming rituals. If they are unduly abstracted, this may be their obsessive thoughts crowding in. They may look tired because their compulsions disturb their sleep. You may notice what seems like excessive tidying, or repeatedly washing coffee cups.

If you are concerned, talk to them in a sympathetic, non-judgmental way. If it's OCD, they will already be suffering exaggerated responsibility and guilt. Don't sound critical. This is an illness.

They may brush you off. It's hard to talk about something that makes you feel like such a bad person. Perhaps chat with someone close to them.

If it seems like OCD, find out all you can about it. Share this advice with your pastoral team or Human Resources staff. Compulsive behaviour is too often a source of mockery. Help others understand the cause.

Assure the sufferer that OCD is an illness, not a personal defect. It's treatable. Create an understanding work and community environment. Support them with prayer.

Christ, who sees every nestling fall,

Make me your instrument to provide a sympathetic and supportive environment for OCD. May I never be guilty of laughing at obsessive behaviour.

Make me a noticing person, who sees the less obvious signs of the disorder. Give me concern for anyone who appears under strain.

Grant me sensitivity as I approach them. Let me do nothing to increase the overwhelming sense of guilt they already bear. Let me hold out the hand of unconditional support.

Let your blessing fall on those who live alongside someone with OCD. It takes a toll on them too. May they also feel themselves upheld in our prayers.

Make me sensitive in how I share this information. I need to ask whether the one with OCD wishes to be named on the prayer list.

Make me an advocate for those with OCD and the organisations supporting them. Help me to share knowledge of this condition, so that we may become a more informed and sensitive community.

ADVOCACY

OCD is not well understood. It is often a source of humour, causing pain to the sufferer. People become impatient with the time-consuming rituals. They may think that meticulously arranging things on a desk gives pleasure to the one who does it. They do not understand the anguish behind this behaviour, the terrible fear that failing in the ritual will cause real harm to others.

Professionals are still learning about the causes of OCD and the best treatment. There are not enough therapists trained in CBT to offer everyone treatment immediately.

All of us need to become better informed about the condition, the suffering it causes, the varied symptoms and the treatment available. We need to be advocates for further research and more therapists.

It is important to talk about OCD and take away the stigma caused by misunderstanding.

We Need to Talk brings together mental health charities, professional bodies and service providers to highlight the need to extend therapies for mental conditions. Many people are still not offered therapy, or have to ask for it. We Need to Talk advocates equality between physical and mental health.

See Resources for the many campaigning organisations and information available.

Christ, Word made Flesh,

Take our voices and use them in your service.

Make us a community that cares about the challenges to mental health. May we be committed to learning more about OCD and the suffering it causes. Let us speak up for those whose illness is misunderstood, even mocked. Make us advocates for greater understanding among those working alongside someone with OCD or employing them.

May our willingness to talk about it give those with OCD the courage to overcome the shame they feel and to talk about their condition. May we mediate your loving support to them.

Bless the work of We Need to Talk in campaigning for better understanding and resources for mental health therapy. Let our support be a measure of the gratitude we feel for our own good health.

Strengthen the charities who work for OCD, who offer helplines, advice, literature, the experience of fellow sufferers.

May I play my part in a supportive community.

LOOKING AFTER YOURSELF

Living with someone who has OCD is wearing. You try to be patient, but you feel the strain as they endlessly go through their checking routines before you can leave the house. They may disturb you at night, as they repeatedly get up to make sure they haven't left electrical equipment on. They may constantly need your reassurance about an obsessive fear.

However much you love them, this can get you down. You need relief. Make sure you get out on your own and do things you enjoy. Don't feel guilty. You will come back refreshed and better able to cope with the problems.

It's normal to feel frustrated, helpless, angry, overwhelmed. Don't blame yourself. There are support groups for friends and families. It helps to share your problems with other people in this situation.

Look after your physical health. Good food, exercise and rest are doubly necessary when you are living under stress.

Relaxation techniques may help: mindfulness, yoga, and many others.

There is One you can always take your problems to in prayer.

The more you learn about OCD, and how best to cope with it, the more confident you will feel about your response.

Christ, my Friend,

I feel guilty about bothering you with my own needs. I'm well aware that it is the one I care about who chiefly needs your help. I'm grateful that I don't suffer as they do.

But you see into my heart. I hardly need to tell you how the strain of living with them is wearing me down. I understand the pressures their obsessions put them under. I try to be patient. Sometimes it slips. I snap at them, and then I feel terrible.

Lord, who took your disciples away to the serenity of lakes and mountains, lift me out of this situation at times. Open my eyes to the beauty of your created world. Let me not lose touch with my friends because of the demands of the one I care for. Restore to me a sense of fun.

I need wisdom and calm, the strength not to join in this compulsive behaviour.

Fill me with peace, so that I may give peace to them.

RESOURCES

OCD-UK: www.ocduk.org office@ocduk.org 0345 120 3778. Helpline: 0345 120 3778 support@ocduk.org OCD-UK, Marble Hall (Office 5),80 Nightingale Road, Derby DE24 8BF

OCD Action: www.ocdaction.org.uk office@ocdaction.org.uk 020 7253 5272 Helpline: 0845 390 6232 support@ocdaction.org.uk Suite 506-507 Davina House, 137-149 Goswell Road, London EC1V

Mind: www.mind.org.uk supporterservices@mind.org.uk 020 8519 2122 Helpline: 0300 123 3393 15-19 Broadway, Stratford, London E15 4BQ. Their website includes a list of other helpful organisations for OCD

Beyond OCD: beyondocd.org This Canadian organisation does not deal directly with individual OCD sufferers but has a great deal of wise information.

Printed information is available from most of these charities. This includes leaflets to show to GPs unfamiliar with the condition.

The websites will provide you with details of support groups, online or in your area.

The British Association for Behavioural & Cognitive Psychotherapies (BABCP) keeps a register of accredited therapists. http://www.cbtregisteruk.com/Default.aspx.

Some books to use in conjunction with professional therapy:

Overcoming Obsessive-Compulsive Disorder: A Books on Prescription Title, David Veal and Rob Willson (Robinson) ISBN: 978-1849010726

What to Do When Your Brain Gets Stuck: A Kid's Guide to OCD, Dawn Huebner, illus: Bonnie Matthews (Magination Press) ISBN: 978-1591478058

These pages are left blank for your own prayers.